How to Flit

How to Flit

Mark Francis Johnson

ROOF BOOKS
NEW YORK

ISBN: 978-1-931824-74-3
Library of Congress Control Number: 2017963480

Cover art by Joe DeGiorgis
Back cover author photo by Sarah DeGiorgis

For Sarah DeGiorgis

Grateful acknowledgment is made to the editors of the journals in which some
of these poems first appeared: *Supplement*, *Fanzine*, and *Social Text*. Many thanks
to Sarah DeGiorgis, Lawrence Giffin and Aaron Winslow for help with the
manuscript.

NEW YORK
STATE OF
OPPORTUNITY. | Council on
the Arts   This book is made possible, in part, by the New York
State Council on the Arts with the support of
Governor Andrew Cuomo and the New York State Legislature.

Roof Books
are published by
Segue Foundation
300 Bowery, New York, NY 10012
seguefoundation.com

Roof Books
are distributed by
Small Press Distribution
1341 Seventh Street
Berkeley, CA. 94710-1403
800-869-7553 or spdbooks.org

Contents

TNT smiled. "Yes," he said. "Very."

—*Pierre Rey*

.

200, 300 or 400 Volts

Overcritical public the

delight you take in seeing me

conscious

of, of an inability to do
it right —

or to do it right again, or
again and again maybe —

to do   justice to the SLAB charm of my subject,
  a prickle historic

200, 300 or 400 volts — this

delight is 200, 300
400 volts dread ministered
  to by one
outspent, milk-livered, whose luf is gauze dressings
nothing like what's on Pat's back.

Will I come back personally with the part? YES
  it will
  be nothing, like
  what's on Pat's back,
there's nothing like what's on Pat's back

out there, no

  thing

worse. I will come back

you fought what's on Pat's back and won.
Won me the part!

316 Dollars

Old before — then
who had 600
could see "bxr" go down,
6000
brine 600's grin.
Now, old again

some of the mountains are jeweled or made

of a jewel
So

<u>rookery relocation notes</u>

Cheap Sub-Heavens | maybe
Building Electronic Pad | maybe
Each Fam Lives By Itself In The Heart Of Wood X | no fam
Contiguous Territories 30 & 31 | may|be
Colloidal Silver Conference Call | 800's a crowd
Contemporary Caper I | *no waste disposal, couldn't leave*
Resting Easy | pod + Bron = ?
Rhythm Worker | if they'll halve me
Contemp. Caper II | *nothing succeeds like no waste disposal*
Mellow Mood | $$$$$$$$$
Starting Line | can't go home etc.
Summer Refresher | what's gorse again?
Midge-Place | 2 crowds (one human) into which...
Cheap Sub-Heavens | again maybe
Soft Sell | sure!
Hold On Just A Little While Longer | no

4172693000

A few words at this point may

not be

amiss: four
one

seven two six

nine three zero zero

zero. Two rings of wood or iron

remain in contact with each other
time, but vortex-rings will not, not vortex-rings
vortex-rings

beat each other away as two
spinning fops will do

if they touch ever so gently

A Few Groundlings

Half a few
of what groundlings,
this at least I thought
we knew

Saw it in a holo | first loaf here
on the eve of assuming the surface pop
consists of nobles and their cultivars
The conversation 1 Gary Thrater had

food, air!
can you share me How many tones
stone that you want to process per hour? and
what the final product size you need after crushing

this pod, in its way arrestingly sumptuous
NOT a mysterious sport of nature. There's a fat
fat-fur train *hunting by racing* hunted peops, 580
become 400, 400 forty, and our forty, four

A Fortnight of Nerves

A fortnight of nerves but one, two
  good hours indoors

the wet day, winning by bettering

Accounts of the Rexels
Accounts of the Revels

those revels these
FIXING their book feet from
—separated by a wall, yes—

the young world Colwynox,

                                    where

the earliest reference to the head
is yet to come—tomorrow's revels.
In 50 years the export market for tomorrow's revels
imagine!

:::

Against quaint illustrations a "dog" has "had"
see a "fly" counterpoised, head...

A Gassy Maid

Said particle laid on air
thinking of cooked things

recently cooked, like a saint

adverting to cures, *they never took*
The granary barbarians' brief
to come back to life, yes, and
this time finish it off with care but also,

  also drama, played
on a finger of medicine across wet boxes
NOT FREE FOOD

  Dream,
Bron, of food in dry boxes

of food in dry boxes dream
particle, recent convert to predation

come back and hold yourself and see how you like it
off today with dissolution booming
NO FREE FOOD

A Guess at the Riddle

How do I put the sprig back? This NEED
Falsified telegraphic news prime source

the use of 120 men here | area | 120
122 each a mediator of disputes, an example to youth
These figures are, regrettably, not misleading

imbecilic self-indulgence
sense

data. This very need, however, holds out promise
I will guess right

how do I turn the spring back
how do you turn on First

Years crisp and clear video ba

A Small, Healthy Breakfast

Too pink black figs

relieving oneself in the bath most fearful

DREAM FREE FOOD NOW!

Curious | suddenly | to witness the act at close range

that is, to invite an education I'd long wished to avoid,
I smied, smied, protected as I was by shrubbery

over which I could see nothing and knew it.
Consolation helps those in trouble, if speaker is

trustworthy (t-shirt

idea)

Absence Reduction as Play

I don't know his title, use

        Doke

or Porcelain Thane.
What do you think the absence,

do you think the absence reducer
Doke
or Porcelain Thane has

thingwise? Not a rubber
nor a stick, nor anything of the kind
  it is freebies. Freebies
—the simplest reward method possible—

ensure he is notified within 24 of losses, info
proper to his immediate needs yet overused,

insufficient, maybe fawn

gray. When

absence reducer Doke or Porcelain Thane feels

he will go find the bank where he left it
last frolic; then he will shake, so moved!

and then shake the bank as if to shake

bread out, a non-change of habit
related to SECURITY that has triggered

new habits.

Alertness as a Stooge

Whitish patches against low-lying black hills

FFMH

FFMH humps a sewer pipe

Alertness as a stooge, even that would be fine.
I spend my savings at Fletcher's False Medical History. Waving
the sheaf of papers I've acquired I race into the low-lying black
hills, stop in a white *puddle* and wait. Twenty mule teams burn up
the wires to your office. I am trying, with Fletcher's False Medical
History's pricey help, to extort compassion from a potential
supernatural protector.

Playing with my long sleeves

would be

a better use of my

afternoon.

Altered U-Knit Promo Kit

Hadn't yet given up charging
a small headful of mesh—
the humiliation of that sorcery,
huffing a folded blue towel,
We Knit You
now

U-Knit, the wretch Ing
catacombed by inattention
how savagely could be harrowed and still function
anticipating failure to find a good place later

#################
****

two assholes never slept conceiving D
it

two assholes never slept conceiving Dit
while | Atlantis sank beneath the sea,

while Atlantis sank beneath the sea
two assholes never slept | conceiving D

it
charged a headful of mesh 100.

An Intermediate Form

Was it really only 45
  or 4 or 5
wind blowing past a Camp in daylight
an intermediate form
or was I there too

IN MY MINI-WAY

as

a munching with great pleasure on roasted "neatness", some 70
kinds

precision I never used self-organizing
and now will

never use?

Animule

    The dense
columns of UNCLE SON carbon

out of ev'ry nut bowl rise!
    putting legs on the bowl is fair

if we could but wipe a roast chicken, a fruit bowl

of disc

arded blueprint paper to which "a nose can be added"
would not seem THE

animule.
One cold and stormy night I dreamed I was eating shredded
wheat biscuits, and I bit my moustache off

woke, and stared at the pyro-cord
right there in the candy bowl all along.

So cold I threw a log on the air-conditioner.

Anxious Post-Ex

As if on the squally wind, a maxim blew into my mind

"A fit of sickness gives a most excellent chance of throwing off any bad habit, if its possessor be really anxious to set it adrift."

This, *this* was the light in which I would view my post-existence!

My bad habits were multiform:

1) I had never seen a horse and knew nothing about them, yet frequently opined, when "cornered" and waspish, that a young, spirited one imparts a portion of that vital energy with which it overflows to a dull, melancholy, weakminded rider.

2) I had never seen a horse and knew nothing about them, yet frequently opined, when "cornered" and waspish, that a young, spirited one imparts a portion of that vital energy with which it overflows to a dull, melancholy, weakminded rider.

3) I had never seen a horse and knew nothing about them, yet frequently opined, when "cornered" and waspish, that a young, spirited one imparts a portion of that vital energy with which it overflows to a dull, melancholy, weakminded rider.

4) I had never seen a horse and knew nothing about them, yet frequently opined, when "cornered" and waspish, that a young, spirited one imparts a portion of that vital energy with which it overflows to a dull, melancholy, weakminded rider.

5) I had never seen a horse and knew nothing about them, yet frequently opined, when "cornered" and waspish, that a young, spirited one imparts a portion of that vital energy with which it overflows to a dull, melancholy, weakminded rider.

6) I had never seen a horse and knew nothing about them, yet frequently opined, when "cornered" and waspish, that a young, spirited one imparts a portion of that vital energy with which it overflows to a dull, melancholy, weakminded rider.

7) I had never seen a horse and knew nothing about them, yet frequently opined, when "cornered" and waspish, that a young, spirited one imparts a portion of that vital energy with which it overflows to a dull, melancholy, weakminded rider.

Ars Poetica

from Richard Dadd's "Elimination of a Picture and Its Subject"

Fancy was not to be evoked
From her etherial realms
Or if so, then her purpose cloaked
And nuzzling the cloth, on which
The cloudy shades not rich,
Indefinite almost unseen
Lay vacant entities of chance,
Lent forms unto my careless glance
Without intent, pure fancy 'tis I mean
Design and composition thus—
Now minus and just here perhaps—plus—
Grew in this way—and so—or thus,
That fairly wrought they stand in view.

Part from the shades designed
Part a vain fancy, all inclined
A common end to gain
Of nothing something still
To stand before, the sight to fill
Something we have, having, we
Yet have not
Be it so or nay, why care a jot?

Bank Rat

Saw, heard

and spoke for half an hour, the next day

her sense of smell vanished, on the

24th hands closed

                around a cudgel—

and there is another more or less authenticated story,
yes

of a bank rat hulling globular

crap

watched from the future by other bank rats
trapped the next fall, winter and spring.

Better Than All This

Rubbishy thoroughfare, slick of fat
blackenings | softenings | "home"

  etc.

::::

I hope the next world's drains
are square

hope
if they're not I don't care,

in *that* storm sluice
down one, whatever shape—

better than all this, than anything—me!
a bald wand of asphodel rescued from Pompeii.

And what does my name tag say
in that dimension which is *dimensiony?*

I EXPECT YOU KNOW YOURS.

Bleat

Six pills drawn as pink aerosol.

The way a warrior would beat an ox if
his word-hoard had the blahs. One evening
bleats

a statue the way a warrior

would
if his word-hoard had the blahs. One
is happiest when all becomes gel.

Beneath a vertical gray cracker left blank

electricity

spoilt

Claims

Eleven chevrons
of geese had

passed overhead in
as many

hours. False. Nine
in quite ragged formation but he

had tried as hard to join the
ragged as the fine. False

Colwynoxians

As products of gloom they start

and start and start and start, some
"gather twitches 'til a choate shiver's made"
it can be sold off-world

where what moves moves because gone.

War yields linguistic oddities —
no penalty for wasting treat exceeds mush of said

up in one's head

Cooks and Officers

I gratefully acknowledge Mrs. Horace Cook
without whom she

would not be mentioned in this book.
Oh, how I wish some great shipwreck would scatter

a lot of this person here, so that we
could easily look at her extraordinary shapes fit

officers.

Cox South

To kill the fams of every exec
at FFMH famous for
"bellowing" and "howling" or
awaiting a radiant flood of Tower

ounce of farce in advance to squander
here, in the heavy wealth of these itless woodlands,

food | factory | lock.
Be wise when I am wise!
My great hope,

                        merit in the

admiration of virtue!

Remote prenatal day as water

no sure sea-marks visible Bus 40

brief terrene comradeship

Crisp Young Balls

Stop in a little rosy cleft to be
crisp young balls—

prepared to get luncheon, my fanny's immediate future at
stake—

prepared to get luncheon, my fanny's immediate future at stake,
I stop in a little rosy cleft to be

crisp young balls at play

OR SO
I say. But no

am here considering in its moral,

social and sanitary aspects my plastic shed
9 feet by 5 in width, where seven persons slept, and six

now sleep,

the greater part of the Dog-row

moments before we received the foul contents of a single ditch
and, within seconds, began to die off, all of us laughing at the vast
voice blaring out of the sky from every direction with *advice*—

BUY STEEL

Day 427

Only on 426 days of my life did I look upon
a buddy like mine's instruction

    sheet

...pacing foster-dawn, recorded by eternity's cam...
...maintenance of this one affinity whilst evading
tons of train...

  Certainly NER | VES
measured without corn my pain,
above long gulf of liquid darkness rocked by

mini A mirage

involved in the calamity of confused and spraying
                            poles. Poorb

ores.

After disassembly I
play like leverets on the lawn

Discovery 3 Passes Through 4

Six weeks of immersion
folded diagonally, bits at the rear
—yet until today I

thought this the lunchwagon.
Nearly over

tedious and arbitrary cluster of behavior lessons!
Light detection and motility

eyespots in duplicate sets of ghee

plant supervisor

why does it work? It doesn't work
no. 3 passes through no. 4
and when he sees a bunny hanging

up, he, without the least compunction, appropriates it to himself,
by right of discovery. Other magical activities
hitherto prevented me from acceding to his re

rererequest

STOP WORKING IN THE CALL CENTER.

It would not anyway just have been quitting a job, but leaving a
game unfinished. Now

light detection and motility,

eyespots in duplicate sets of ghee

am plant supervisor or

plant supervillain The Wet Blanket

F Rations

Crippled little spheriod super-capsule
unsafe to outlive, the whole body
the WHOLE BODY of a strong people presents

you with
this

old gift certificate gene,
we trillion as one willed it

to be

spliced

into tin can F

enjoy

Flushables

At last editing flesh-tints! We was

an ingredient knot paid cot plus looks

at Spring |
ingredients for use
yes in beautiful pyramids of goo but

also in humid assurances and—per one such—in other flush-
ables as goo(d) | was

just a cough on the battlefield. There there

was | too

Food

Humid field

hospital,

men like fists of molding foie-gras
a dirty little tweed cap the peach

among phantoms. Of H
much

on a cot. *Absences & Silences: Or, A Future Like
A Strange Cheese.* Such visions! But after

it lived no differently, adrift until eaten...

Food Two

When I came of age I did it
the unthinkable—fled

our pox of little red tents to be
   on

...salt-flats? Were they

salt-flats? The very first day
far, shimmering rubbish

or a beast wept
morphemes big with revelation,
sound preceding smell

The tang of carbolic acid and gangrene's hopeless stink form yet another variant of the musk life seeps to interest death… Once upon a time I discovered a man making love to a cheese, glorying in its many holes; and you have likened my future to a cheese…

Forestless

Explore what in tragedy beaches agents

watch
P explore what in tragedy beaches agents?

:::

  Lord,

the excitement of information precisely conveyed!
We cannot do without it, here

moving uneasily through what, to Q,
seem ranches.

:::

This
rock
rock

Getting Started

Getting started as a flounder
on another world, using jokes about
            piles in the audience

fair if they are medium-size

piles.

Getting started—asking where I find gas,
the answer dividing that alien scrum.

I've been reading the gas file for news,
reading, rereading, reading again & rererereading,
a routine the glows watching call SIT

"just a dog

cashing another world's monkey-cow's check!"

Peach of Marks has its own booth | sells

"Once upon a time, I remember, starting over was like a bright, if
cool, spring day. Now, after so many false starts, it is not even like
a bright winter's day, but like a dream of spring from which you
know you must soon awaken, as before, and which has grown less
intensely bright and green and bracing with every repetition, as
though you were dreaming it through a thickening scrim."

HALF PLAGUE; or, Kinds of Generals

O,
the mismated techniques used to believe it *life*

not a splendid counter-attack
itself constructing
generals on the fly, trillions | result of

fuss with *kinds*

                         of generals—

a material always catching.

:::

One general thus resuscitated
oversaw smooth

dev in the generals'

       powerful framework,
now conceived as mastery and foam.
Another

general, indispensable

lived most of his adult life.
Another general

a bubble.

How Shall I Describe To You What

How shall I describe to you what

        a life it was?

Scenes
Anonymous notary and a dog jump

ambitions, centered wholly in feats, realized
on "a grandly intimate" scale when "sailors" die
  nearby

—the dog enjoying this as extra grooming
the notary as interesting obiter dicta—

November
"Willow crowns" and "gifts" and "kisses"
  a crop of technical slang
right usage a game not worth

                  the
"candle"

Gaslit world where no little feet echo
abandoned for Colwynox where "playfellow" means
toe's corresponding toe
Scenes

How the Rooster Got Its Sports

But I don't want to wait, Wisteria
Wisteria from Ash Bing Machinery,
"*improving our motto*" a long day heaving sports!
A long day heaving sports at

                    a crusher I am in

training to assume is otherhomely
chanticleer
in poop hat

transfigures us —

Night-sweats fed
the fen, his bed.
Big, silent birds
looked in

—and amongst the birds, Bron—

How to Flit

They
They take

holos of your loved ones and play
Day's Most Broken Boddy w/

beasts from other dimensions playing

games all their own.

Meagre dinner of odors,
Papie Wapsie,
you know that this song
maked me always crie,
becouse it tought how it should be,
whene i would lose you, you see !!
And look now where we are !!
You are really gone ,
You loved everything aboud the sae and the

beautiful ships !!!
This is my song to you !!
Your litle boy Bronny !!!xxxxx
One day only contrived to sink in

Instruction and More Instruction

The persons of old people especially
sometimes contain spots void
of sensibility. An
apparatus   after it's cared for itself!!   is

told, *After you've cared for yourself*
   again, exploit these. There *is*

indifference, which is a "size" for this

apparatus. One end of the box is

loaded with dried peas told
   run down this

tortuous passage. The professed prickers
use a pin the point or lower part of which is

on being pressed down, sheathed in
   the upper, which is

hollow for the purpose, and that which
appears to enter the body dis

not pierce it at all.

****

What loaf in a cavity on earth?

One morn
observe a festive drain operation

using acupuncture anaesthesia at
the Worker-Peasant Social.

"Can I move my legs a little?"
"I don't know, can you?"

Introvision Sample 3: "Too Late"

Years after ONE
quiet sleep, "my food is prophetic dreams
of eating dreams"

, it found

itself just bare, shaking

frost-bitten buttocks and a swollen knob—

and a head—

"hygiene: an apt. in the Human Wisdom complex"

crummy
last words, roared moments before it pushed back the heavy
mane of forcefield from its crown, having fatally mistaken the
pounded strip for a very large bed covered with a smooth rubber
sheet in dark blue—

mistaken it convulsively, with jerks—

Kinds of Pockets

A starship laden with diapers

    what is a diaper but a pocket

yes — I guess — a kind

  of pocket

a starship laden with giftwrap.

After those

two never

another.

More Tidings of Counsel

Now I wish to indicate to you
or you, not you

the condition of my abdomen | it is

a hull emblazoned!

TWELFTH SUCH.

On the twelfth
Such instructed me not to bathe,
and the same on the next day, and the day after

that; I passed the time in

talking about my 'jamas and in games.

Later, I bathed at evening

at dawn had pains in my abdomen,
as pain spread over a right side
I saw grown men
taking milk in pure shining air good for travel!

Necessary Services; or, Scarred Ports

Every few
years, perhaps
at regular
intervals—of that
I am not certain—
while gnawing a small springy

bog stick out of
sight of creatures, I obtain necessary services

  promptly.

But I know
it can't last, someday

I'll be seen to have healed

  ports.

No More Hand For a Pillow

Ancient protocols, validated by time, work
                             as engines—

rent out your head or   sell

it if

that's a lip. Your MOM should have
  kept the stork.

Who can't help the way it haunt food

seven stars!—

Overhear pup

adjusting, "I saw his

hut in his pocket"
as if he had the clothes,

hut, utilities paid, a joke fried egg

Honorary shelter   it's a thought

and the echo of gears a gangway into the night.

No Prunes

Hygiene holidays, a single affiliation fee—
it would be wrong to revive it
Delicately organized citizens, please

      elect a quiet   ing room

undisturbed by particles how hard,
night corpuscles largely dropped

      out a Mind.

I settled back to get my bottom deep into

the tub where warm water would
soothe and relieve the ache; in a kind world

one does

not need xrust

apple cores, prunes, scraps

of carrots, potato peel, cabbage leaves

  to

squeeze themselves in a merry row
delicately organized, soon to be gone.

Delicately organized, soon to be gone
it would be wrong to revive me!

Nongolfer

What
It's a joke nongolfer—a recusant—showering

half the mist panic

he, it, he, nongolfer

won't remember marveling
the wildebeest, motionless
months, out of its plastic depths could heave

three toy steps now that the elephant, knocked aside by his towel,
no longer blocked its way. This penniless recusant nongolfer, *this*
penniless recusant nongolfer, won't remember asking himself:
What do you feel regarding the urgent endeavor you're under-
taking today for luf? But he's the very very poor, let's just say the
very poor, recusant nongolfer who will remember remembering
another four a.m. shower taken seven years earlier *without* hope,
he's the, he's the very very poor recusant nongolfer

trying not to look like
a strained hair in a can. Well
well, what is *this*, four years

away from appearing on his skin??

Nongolfer Two

Not to say

a shower

can't function as a monotonous environment, capable of
producing monotony of impressions and intellectual drowsiness.
Limitation of voluntary movements by relaxation of the
muscles—you can see how easily

this is

accomplished in a shower. And fixation of the attention? The
showerhead or, even better, the drain, serve as excellent foci.
Limitation of the field of consciousness however requires an
as-if-expanded effort. Here we introduce the priest-hole, nominated
earlier as a perfectly monotonous environment for those not
hiding. Think about a priest-hole while you're in the shower.

Not More Instructions

A young runaway

utt, I "wanted" to show by lack of hair
around my phony smile that

...it was cold.

I was on the Holovision last night. I'll sleep
  anywhere when I'm drunk.
I follow the horses, and so do the horses that I follow.

I was on the Holovision last night. I'll sleep
  anywhere when I'm drunk.
I follow the horses, and so do the horses that I follow.

I was on the Holovision last night. I'll sleep
  anywhere when I'm drunk.
I follow the horses, and so do the horses that I follow.

I follow the horses, and so do the horses that I follow.

Nth Anniversary of Pocketing My Hut

Today it would be as difficult to find a hut
a huthold rather in which one or

one member could not give a lucid, fair
distinction between volt and ampere

as to find the hut outside of which
a trapper discovered
in a deadfall these

stones and chunks

responsible for the failure of the middle-class to inculcate the
principles of self-help in the poor and at the same time ward off
snow and sleet from interfering with its (the middle-class')
workings. 2187, I hadn't yet been forced—or rather, convinced
of the wisdom of a "compromise", as in 98, 99 or 100—
to pocket my hut

O stones and chunks

you *know* obscurely "at some level" how I miss it

here on the street, organ gridding

have a good appetite though… eat what my pinky nail collects…
in fact there are only two things I can't eat for breakfast—lunch

& dinner

Number 7

Gave away woe in a form
old crap, emerging from
apparently livable hole to puzzle
beings I would | not know

a special ref *compliments of your hospital*,
soup spoon with a bell attached, two wooden blocks
  A and B
place fly on block A, strike smartly with B.

My kingdom for an effortless bowel movement
just to be a regular guy
If I work one week tonight
Special Situation No. 7: You have to move

huge object first, in order to work.
More than anything miss my foot

ing.

Turkey Day

Turkey Day
in one far corner grows a mass "not at home"

4 glorified screw-eyes hold us in place, both grateful that's
an interior wall next act, everybody but the Turkey grateful
I work early.

Occasional Blockag Suc

: : : : : : :

Without whatever it is, the years
the sick decide to picture medical supplies,
sicker become pictures

of medical supplies. Something here is like

that still, totaled tractor spreading *Excellence*.
Stable work history

as matter.

"Occasional blockag suc" less or more

than "infrequent blockage suc"? More

more

more

On Fun

Live
a little as twin fogs,
return to the space bar after my shift.
Why did I Shirley say it, can I just please
   swing shitwork?
HATE YOU *Giant Bug Pensi*

on Fun

d | As for the empire, once wet hounds, I Shirley

mash underheel my favorite sweet, a King in chunks

   past my plastic shed flare
olive and blue, and bluer   and black

leaves,
sold wrinkled photos of *that sea*

On Imnibus

On Imnibus, next its maudlin rotor

sick, but not silent, windows all

tight as wax for the unfant's sake, and and and

you, tearing your throat to rags, abortive efforts to call

a person who has just left everybody

"white caps cut from construction paper"

the hull red paper, the sails, white

Other Turkeys

Our black ebony "wand"

enjoyed our itch

We six enjoy being

esp.

being examined at a distance.

Pease

First go I to the bottom of the seas

                                  there
   the weather being wet
explain the singular of pease

is pease.

Then home to my plastic shed
lil ½ bed

/

It is but a toy I give me, this instruction scrap

8 unnumbered pages
divided into 4 sections

qui parvum contemnit, indignus est magno
hee that refuseth a little kindness

is unworthy of a greater

Piffle: Action and Aftermath

Use two

tubes, or the same

tube twice at the same time.

...
...
...
...
...

Done!

.

Finding himself down to the last hit of rice —
tube crushed up and thrown aside —
so much easier than calling it home —

man's poor hope: Byb

Player Characteristics

—as a buddy leapt a brilliant wood
of glucosacks and ballsy wren's eyes,
the best road through it **DROX**, a floor...
shining in the distance, not far, we saw—
and so disbanded—
and having been here now two decades
and a year

still, still in the confusing streets
the fantastic, subdued alarm
of this queer city I sometimes see
a familiar face atop
a buddy like mine,
and wonder—what?
It was so long ago now
I patted my pockets for a light.

Playgoing Result for MISS ION

All sold agree
  much sadness in the life of
this trustworthy cream figure.
Where it's face had been a kind of entrance
  now

interior visible. I saw an old statue with downcast eyes,
I worshipped it roughly: it
  gifted me the slipper

off its—how—unbroken foot: I was leased by the honor

                soon celebrated
buying at random a cheap snap

decision to rein

terpret MISS ION.

No, I give up.

Pressure

Waking, it is

desolate it is not angry

"over its tears' foul taste it wept"

                                   Pressure

again to be a gnome, the better to have
some ill-defined influence on the fun's issue.

PRESSURE | PRESSURE

Infected cigarillo burns need it! the

  hide

                         •

gulls dining heartily on castaway gnome

Reading Group Miracle

—as performed by Yum Yums 123—

How

is it a sweetcorp history squeezed

of all the

all the juicy parts

reads as good fiction,

having reached chapter

eight are we

too restructuring

soon will pair off??

yum yum

yum yum yum yum

yum yum. Yum Yums 123

Reservations

Then, he leaves like Squill

In, a struggle Patch's
eye was grazed, forcing him to wear a patch *again*

the size and color of the toot apparently
the solitary effort in

                              this direction.

Does Squill's

transient
uncertainty strike when

we turn to another plant rsvd,

the worm on it

  rsvd too

—for a turkey rsvd?!

Riches Wasted on the Eld

Paper money chewed into a cud
stuck to a wall serves nicely as a peg

,

—

hang

amatory sketches. Now I cannot afford
ONE erotic mezzotint

depicting this

peg! When your hair

has turned to silver, I'd like to be your barber

  the
solution.

Robinson Pre-Ball; or, Moments of New Foam

What a proud stain on this glittering hall,
chlamydomonas reinhardtii! Uses lufly blue light,
a cue to control its sexual life cycle program—
very like how the Robinson Pre-Ball

shares foam. What

right here with you, short and explosive, who
  invented the 20 foot pole
and you, a substantial clinical entity, who
  invented the 30 foot pole
and you, a linen maid in a religious house, who
  invented the 40 foot pole
and you, soon to be refusing FREE FOOD, who
  invented the 50 foot pole

and you, fond of fishing, who
                    married your dog

"it had worms."

This is blooming behavior! Wait
blooming behavior!
the yard is enormous, the dome so small.
Today is unlucky, you will probably lose
a Fist Instruction Sheet where floats

"the past"

Sanitary Ramblings: Alpha Row

Today we're looting a row of new houses, Alpha-Row
and we are experimenting   O

ne child selects a picture of a small pool of pasty putrescent filth
to recall the word "winner". When asked why she chose the
picture, she gives the perfectly satisfactory answer, "Because once
I beat a small pool of pasty putrescent filth." And she elaborates,
"It all started with hello, on an evening long ago."

However, only one day later, while staring straight at the picture,
she is unable to recall the word "winner", thinks loudly, "-r??"

EVERYBODY   CAN   HEAR   HER

As a necessary excretory product of this breakdown (itself a
valuable result) chemical nostalgias are produced—but not in
the child! Listen, however, to the investigators

"Hello, I don't even know your name. But I'm hoping all the
same this is more than just a simple hello."
"Hello. Do I smile and look away? No, I think I smile and stay,
to see where this might go."

Score for Frame

Score for frame pic
of Theralyze & Finance
amazing lice the
only way, by living.
                      Are a
contry star. Is he shaking his head
or is his head just shaking

remembering a safe exploded from within by
shade, how it sponsored the copse, "temporarily"
dooming clover, drowning the lit
basket of a male picnicking alone?
              | Stress divides
waif into colony of mushrooms who
sleep standing up the better to

exit dreaming

Scrap of Gelastic Leather

A scrap of gelastic leather squeaks

lines cut from an

earlyish

holo in which, too new

not to turn blue

outdoors coatless in December, it

mimed a voiceover bit:

**** *** ** *** *** ***** *** ********* ****
  ** *****

What it feels now has the same motivational profile
  as pain.

Season's Graftings

How are you this Fine Frosty? OK NEED

admit holiday insertion
prompted disquis on holes

need

a shoe company—shoe company—shoes—shoes—sell shoes
myself—men's shoes, women's shoes, boys' shoes, girls' shoes,
babies' shoes, working men's shoes, working babies' shoes,
slippers, you bet

in the street I distinguished a fart from a fabriolet.

I was

.a scarlet-at-graft-sites manager
.could not live up to my contract
.so they abandoned the idea
.and stayed home all the best of winter.

Fine Frosty mornings! NEED

Series of Twelve

Long sunny days in a punt,
twelve

experimental testing of the dew, or not, or not

put a paper hat on—

isn't the "ground" of all this

carpeted with the golden
blooms of the little wild Rock

Rose, do we not know that flower to be

a remedy for terror?

Sketch of Colwynoxian Mistakes: 1

Superseded by others of more modern type
past generations accumulate by radio—in hotels—or by telephone
—in bars or clubs—to discuss migraine ("Dost thou miss them?"
"Yea, with all my head"), the piteous useful fiction of a hunter in
their midst, the overdue revival of Volapuk.

One day
with sudden gross animality they
immortalize Ignatz

Ignatz who never lived here

Slipper

To sex up a dome arrange a nap with

any big doc-shredder whose technique
was named for—what else?—a barely bee, a barely bee
very famous, built where dad, Ed, fought.
My mother was gravid while there. I thought

as much,—

Ed misheard the barely bee's name,
Sipper not Slipper, Sipper Sipper.

I was Ed

who nobody agreed to be

Some Tableaux

Here, here and

—owing to the hot ray trained on it—
pinguid and so

of use, rubs grooved
wooden wheels until they tell
the joke "Talking Teeth"

humanely. Gazelle

bored with placid country life, tear off

the top of your neighborhood grocer,
return to your vehicle, sick. This
tube you halve pleads—both halves plead—
  tableaux be saved

why

arse-cheeks through pantelettes

ninety plastic aircraft and a cornflake

6 big cobras… and one of them is deaf.

6 big cobras think

our linen will be cleaner if
we put it aside for the fight.

Can your boss help me get a new sef.

Sot Futures Rematch

Here is a problem from far off Und
left message, left message
need help, left message
very ready for treatment
not resting easy on my trailer hitch
eight foot in the well, won't swim an hour

will

work with case management
A blob is   tested
  is blob
these goddamn fumes
ARE IN FACT
Eye Surgeons of Springfield
YOU'VE BEEN HERE FIVE WEEKS
IMPORTANT FOR MEDICAID

Think I shall show box
is empty, that is, you think it is empty, but I saw

some atom
moving around, and sure enough, it is a larger silk—

pardon me, I have it just over here

Success Late in Life

Somehow he has a coat

  has a coat and gets
on his coat while he flees after cursing

me, then somehow quits
the accepted five senses

  inches ahead of

ANOTHER seeking "bits".

:::

So, do we call it

success late in life?? Not at

all

no | for

I discovered this lufly old fan's

bile to be sweet!

Sunshine Part 2: Super Touch

Blobs try, fail—one leapfrogs

ties to a pastoral landscape.
Finally the bottom rock—this rock—gets
classified as attraction. A million
years pass. Nobody left understands

"super touch" was
NOT a messenger's slimy feel and THAT

made

it super.
"And then the sun cried out

to its ray come
home,

give us a chance."

Ray knew it was the main attraction and kept
up a jog.

Tale of the Hiatus

Assume a hiatus
The rise of the first

gang, *The Likeliest Means*

then letters patent, invention of; assume
    dependence on good versions

of

TALE OF THE HIATUS

simultaneously to manifest
and——why not??——become insupportable.
Those caught alone in

anechoic mash, Circumstance——booted
through numberless holes in a cheese's
worst parts, jeers plugging their ears, no idea
how to flit, no thought of flitting——they

should expect this
just, hooted charge to flatter them: "

A commonplace defence
is unsuited for private corresp

ond
ence!

,,

That Little Pit

Hoping ON that pyramid after 21 years to want
to cry

let me see those fights again,
I'm willing if you're willing too,

oh what a feeling.
Oh what a feeling

briefly to be allowed
yet more briefly to want to cry

ON that pyramid
This little pit!

The Game Called "Sot Futures"

Sot Futures

Perform hand hygiene where
  it can see you

Bron, with every spin
you can win
FREE FOOD
How to play | Sot Futures

Perform hand hygiene
because, Bron

No doubt this is a realer heart
and vascular center now

it won.

The Joy of Seeming

After one hour a "white sun" fell

out of my can

burnt the synthetic moly log
we probably don't need to slice until T-day
even in that shit

state it

                    remains

useful for the future

solution of the metaphysical problem
I give my time. O log,
craved by lasers. My discarded self

glories to the joy of seeming, of seeming

   where, oh
                    in an
old holo. *Look,*
us. Anyhow

burnt synthetic moly smell's my new self!

The Lie

Abusing the team "stress meter" alone
I learn, O Colwynox, andirons
and some three rushlight holders
apple scoops of bone, behavior axes
chats on bargains while racing cloverleaf
  traffic circles

—the stuff of life I had planned on grieving
come Emigration—

dissolved the morn a plasma cannon
arrived on my shedstep: my ID.
Now I am given a gatling laser! That old grief

pings as if sent through a Hayseed transmitter
wailed in a language reliant on gesture—

I do not feel what I knew—

so, this is home.

The Wonder Of It

Day approacheth
am selling powers

and wig and cry. I sold my powers and wig. Cry,

echo throughout the Wood!
infection of the voice
selling the wonder of it

or give up, cry—
that glubbing noise that signals
despair of ever not meaning *that.*

What I wanted to say

Nuts we have no hi-res fire.

Cry, echo throughout the Wood!
over-selling the wonder of it all.

Rent day

Thunder Cue

Four teeth left. One

dirtbag of many, trees and houses
painted on us in blue

see us through

graphic enhancement.
Four teeth. I believe in my pursuers, BUT

occupying my foster-space believe I
or my

pursuers went off, in some drainage ditch
collect extra self over time.

Boss loves a great pop!
Pop loves a great boss!

Toast

The joys

of Half Half-Day, unknown

to those

present. Form

artificial fraternal ties

Try at Cottages

A down and out starship captain

"phones" in a faun
uses the lawn
"phones" in a man
uses the can.

SUM Papa's research will extend considerably the already grand
limits of the starship captain's system, show him he wants

2 pretentious, well-kept cottages.
These

2. We are looking forward to

it being too late.

Two Excellent Jobs

Flakes of show disentangle
appearing as the audience
good job
No

definite dimensions for that

fell instrument,
it does everything

too. Is not necessary a glucoshade be
sharply defined: wouldn't be so in reality

"a brain being always eight or ten feet"

off the waiting room. Reduced gentle-folk!
You seem the very

shits for that profession (glucoshade).

Unpreparing for Battle

Two turkeys used in hallways
and on the walls of the cafeteria sat

enjoying
                    "a wet

                                        one"

having mistaken
end for end of
the diagram in
selecting their berth.
A gallant of Elizabot's time

might have complained, if the rushes that strewed the floor of
the banqueting hall, were so much loaded with fones, and other
remnants of the pheast, that he could not approach

two turkeys
as they sat on the dais

having mistaken
the diagram.
But would he have thought it necessary, like a bean of the present
day, that

a boot continually taking in gravel
                            should in summer
give place to a tender foot, the not-better to sack

another closed Automat?

Ver Illud Erat

Willing to work with cost management,
asking for Misty still

  and S-crawling
  tiles

Qualities. I certainly ought to possess them!
Qualities. I certainly ought to possess them!
Qualities. I certainly ought to possess them!

:::

Five weeks now on this limitary parapet,
below me a broad radiance bossed with gloom—

these posthumous confidences, specimens
  of bygone ardor,
may be among my companions in an unseen world,

solitary decipherment of them how I paw there
  at "spring"
instead of 'aving a second thought—

Volt

As-if-electrically

piners link us by sigh to

fee: a mourner's

+ the previously mentioned

dollars 3.

Trade one's tiny sod for volt

what passes for Spring now. Survival

news true when it porks *The*

Age, so dark the dead wear fat,

the oddity of feeling theirs

in public only, bright public

only

Year 317

Frags of low-comedy sound
coalesced above us,

cursed a joke

heard, by most, as a curse, and so were

—or *it was*—

sent away 461 years: 22 years for insulting a W DIT fooder, 400
years for leaking a state secret. Just once a heaping plate of hard-
boiled eggs was placed on the prime breakfast table of the
ETHYL CROUTON, a starship on which they—it—had
booked sausage. Immediately a succession of cheepings was
heard. Fellow prisoners drew back in horror as this entity ate egg
after egg

after egg after egg

despite the cries of the chicks in them,
punishing the whole plate. As if in expiation
Year 317 summer gardens did advertise
"photographs" of pelf—this idolatry ob
enough to stem new onboard vitriol; and indeed

though I was, perhaps, Admiral

she, having turned a complete somersault, knelt over my face,
pressed tight to her belly, my mouth continuing to suck the flow
of the wine, which her now upright position caused to flow out
in a goodly stream.

Yes, Unscrupulous and Ill-Bred

Time does not suffice to more than sketch
today's strictly enforced heat-fast: the futility
   etc.

—barely noticed by the flash guild annalists—

of this this
this this frozen

shit 12

hrs!

I am unscrupulous and ill-bred. Of course I prefer virtuosity to
imagination where endeavors of brevity are concerned. Even so,
you will surely find "bits" you can use

ENJOY

/

with a curse retract my slackening tool.

ROOF BOOKS
the best in language since 1976

Recent & Selected Titles

Roof Books are published by **Segue Foundation**
300 Bowery • New York, NY 10012
For a complete list, please visit **roofbooks.com**

Roof Books are distributed by
SMALL PRESS DISTRIBUTION
1341 Seventh Street • Berkeley, CA. 94710-1403.
spdbooks.org